Level 3 is ideal for
reading confidence ar
to read longer books v

Special feature:

interest and discussion

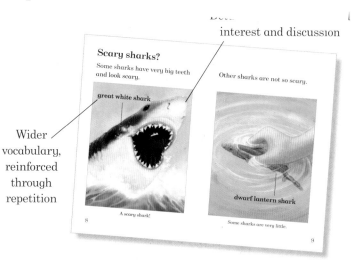

Wider
vocabulary,
reinforced
through
repetition

Scary sharks?

Some sharks have very big teeth
and look scary.

great white shark

A scary shark!

8

Other sharks are not so scary.

dwarf lantern shark

Some sharks are very little.

9

Longer
sentences

Captions and
labels clarify
information

Sharks that hunt

Some sharks, like the
great white shark, hunt
other big sea creatures.

great white shark

Sharks look for food.

10

11

Educational Consultant: Geraldine Taylor
Book Banding Consultant: Kate Ruttle
Subject Consultant: Dr Kim Dennis-Bryan

LADYBIRD BOOKS

UK | USA | Canada | Ireland | Australia
India | New Zealand | South Africa

Ladybird Books is part of the Penguin Random House group of companies
whose addresses can be found at global.penguinrandomhouse.com.

ladybird.com

Penguin
Random House
UK

First published 2015
006

Printed in China

A CIP catalogue record for this book is available from the British Library

ISBN: 978-0-723-29513-6

Sharks

Written by Chris Baker

Illustrated by Daniel Howarth

Contents

Scary sharks?

Some sharks have very big teeth and look scary.

great white shark

A scary shark!

Other sharks are not so scary.

dwarf lantern shark

Some sharks are very little.

Sharks that hunt

Some sharks, like the great white shark, hunt other big sea creatures.

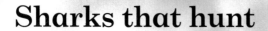
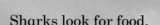

Sharks look for food.

10

great white shark

Sharks find food

Many sharks can see very well.
This helps them find creatures to eat.

The shape of a hammerhead shark's
head helps it to see well.

hammerhead shark

Sharks catch food

When great white sharks see a creature to eat, they can swim very fast to catch it. When they catch food, they bite it.

This shark swims fast!

This shark bites its food with its big teeth.

great white shark

The head helps

The shape of the hammerhead shark's head helps it catch and hold creatures.

hammerhead shark

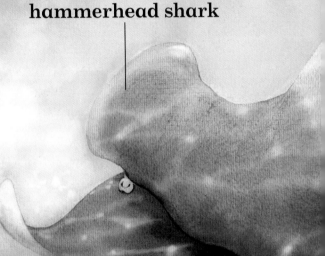

This shark can hold creatures down and bite them.

17

Shark teeth

Great white sharks have many teeth. When a shark's teeth come out, it will get new ones.

great white shark ─────

A shark can get thousands of new teeth!

Shark shapes

Many sharks have shapes that help them swim fast in the water.

mako shark

This mako shark can swim fast.

The great white shark's shape
helps it go fast.

great white shark

This shark does not swim fast.

Basking sharks

Basking sharks are very big.
They might look scary, but
they are not.

Basking sharks do not hunt big sea creatures and they do not bite.

basking shark

Eat, eat, eat!

The basking shark eats little creatures called plankton.

basking shark

Basking sharks do not have big teeth to bite plankton – they just scoop them up.

plankton

Basking sharks' food

Basking sharks are so big that they have to scoop up and eat millions of plankton.

basking shark

Basking sharks eat millions of very little plankton.

plankton

Little plankton look like this.

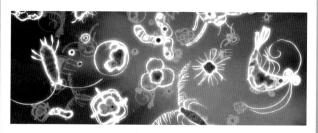

Big and little sharks

Some sharks are big and other sharks are little.

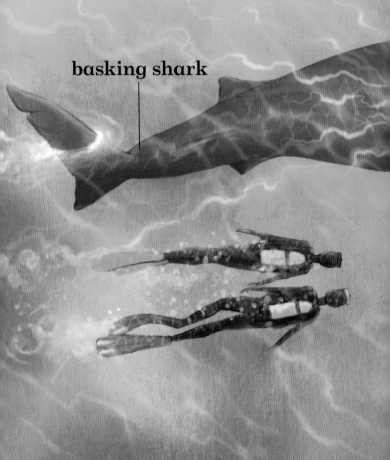

basking shark

The basking shark is VERY big.

The dwarf lantern shark is VERY little.

Glow-in-the-dark shark!

The dwarf lantern shark swims in the dark sea where it can glow in the dark.

dwarf lantern shark

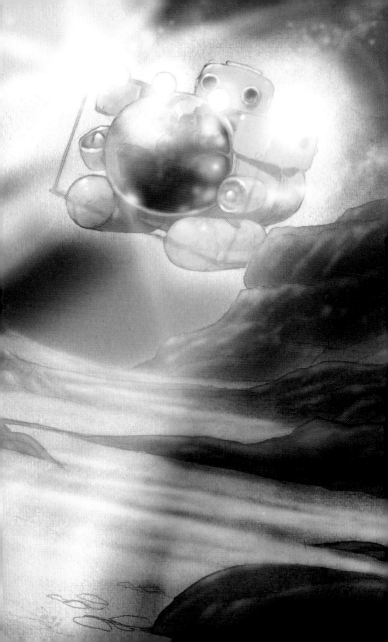

Shark babies

Shark babies are called pups.
Some pups come out of an egg.

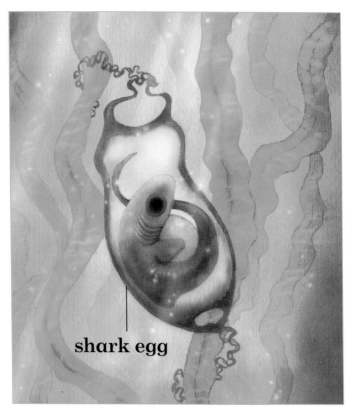

shark egg

This shark pup comes from an egg.

Many shark pups do not come out of an egg. Their mothers give birth to them.

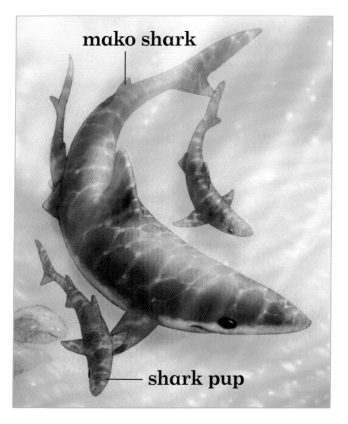

The mako shark gives birth to pups.

Pups look after themselves

When shark pups are born,
they can look after themselves.
They will swim and hunt.

shark pup

These mako shark pups can hunt
when they are born.

Shark journeys

Some sharks go on great journeys.
One great white shark went from
Africa to Australia and back.

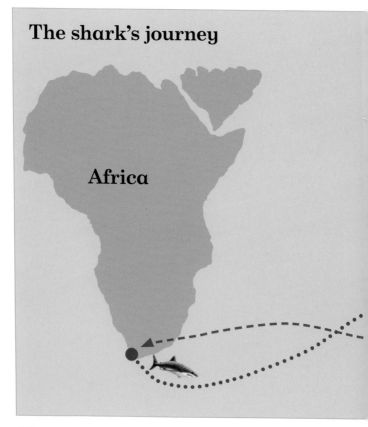

The shark's journey

Africa

The shark went on a journey of nineteen thousand kilometres.

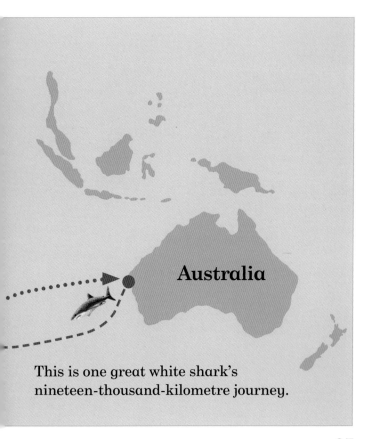

This is one great white shark's
nineteen-thousand-kilometre journey.

Swim, swim, swim!

Many sharks must swim all the time. They can't breathe if they don't swim all the time.

These hammerhead sharks must swim all the time so they can breathe.

Shark attack!

Many sharks attack and eat other sea creatures. But sharks do not often attack or eat people.

Sharks do not often eat people.

Which sharks?

If you went down in the water,
which sharks would you like
to see or swim with?

The scary great white shark.

The big hammerhead shark.

42

The very big basking shark.

The little dwarf lantern shark.

The fast mako shark.

43

Picture glossary

 basking shark

 creatures

 dwarf lantern shark

 great white shark

 hammerhead shark

 mako shark

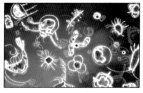 plankton

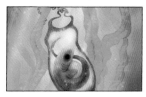 shark egg

 shark pups

 teeth

Index